MAKER MODELS

THEATRE
AND
FILM SET

Anna Claybourne

WAYLAND

First published in Great Britain in 2019
by Wayland
Copyright © Hodder & Stoughton
All rights reserved

Editor: Elise Short
Design and illustration: Collaborate

HB ISBN: 978 1 5263 0741 5
PB ISBN: 978 1 5263 0742 2

Printed and bound in China

Wayland, an imprint of
Hachette Children's Group
Part of Hodder and Stoughton
Carmelite House
50 Victoria Embankment
London EC4Y 0DZ

An Hachette UK Company

www.hachette.co.uk
www.hachettechildrens.co.uk

CONTENTS

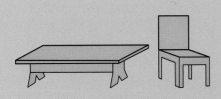
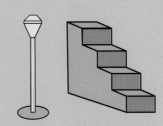

THE STAGE IS YOURS!

Since ancient times, people have put on shows for each other, performing dances, reenacting old tales and creating colourful scenes and spectacles. Gradually, this tradition grew into longer plays performed in theatres, with costumes, sets, props and scenery to help tell a story.

If you love the excitement of theatre, film and TV, and dream of being a backstage whizz or a star of the stage or screen, this book is for you. It shows you how to make a working model theatre, complete with lights, backdrops, props, special effects and even flying harnesses for your actors.

You can put on performances by moving your actors around the stage. Or, if you'd like to make the move into film-making, your theatre can be converted into a movie set for making stop-motion animations, and into a cinema for showing your finished movies!

DO IT YOUR WAY!

You can make a traditional model theatre by following the instructions exactly, but you don't have to. If you prefer, use the instructions as a starting point and come up with your own designs and variations. You don't have to make all the parts of the theatre either. Make a modern theatre in an abstract shape or an old-fashioned round theatre like Shakespeare's Globe. Instead of plays, you could create dance shows, an awards ceremony or a music video for your favourite song. Only one thing really matters – the show must go on!

MAKER MATERIALS

The projects have been designed to work using things you can find at home, like boxes, packaging, and basic art and craft equipment. If you don't have what you need, you can usually get it at a hobby or craft store, supermarket or DIY store, or by ordering online. See page 31 for a list of useful sources.

Charity shops are a great place to look for old, cheap household items and materials, too.

BLOOP BLOOP! SAFETY ALERT!

For some of the projects, you'll need to use sharp tools such as a craft knife or a bradawl (a pointed tool for making holes). Or you might want to use an electric appliance like a hot glue gun.

For anything involving sharp objects, heat or electricity, always ask an adult to help and supervise. Make sure you keep items like these in a safe place, away from where younger children could find them.

CAN I USE THIS?

Before you start emptying the cupboards, make sure any containers or other household items you want to use are finished with, clean and you have permission to use them for your dramatic creation. You're ready to start – let's get this show on the road!

THEATRE AND STAGE

First you are going to build the basic theatre from a large, strong box. As well as a stage, a theatre has a backstage area and the wings, where actors can hide out of sight. Under the stage is the trap room and above the stage is a space called the fly loft.

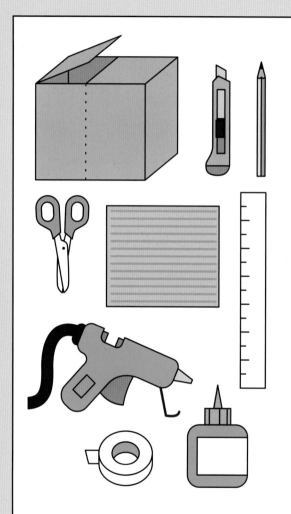

WHAT YOU NEED

- A large, roughly cube-shaped, corrugated cardboard box, no smaller than 30 cm tall and wide
- More corrugated or thick card
- Strong scissors or a craft knife
- A pencil and a ruler
- Strong sticky tape
- Strong glue or a glue gun

1 Start by cutting the top off your box. It needs to be open at the top so that you can control the action inside. Use strong tape to secure any loose joins or bits of card inside.

2 Choose one side of the box for the stage (a wider side, if there is one). With a pencil and ruler, draw a rectangle on the box. Leave space all around it.

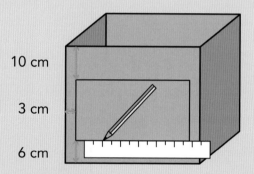

10 cm

3 cm

6 cm

3 Carefully cut along the sides and top of the rectangle. At the bottom, cut the cardboard off about 2 cm above the bottom of the rectangle. Fold the flap inwards.

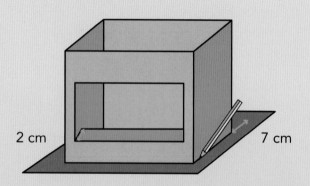

2 cm

7 cm

4 On a piece of thick or corrugated card, trace around the base of the box. Add an extra 7-cm-wide strip along the back.

5 Cut out the shape. Score along the length of the 7-cm strip by running a scissor blade along it, using a ruler. Fold the back flap down. This piece will be the stage.

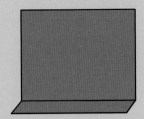

8 Score a line about 2 cm from the top of this shape and fold it over. In the bottom corner of the shape, cut a small doorway, about 7 cm tall.

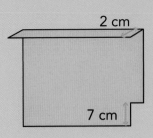

2 cm

7 cm

6 Fit the stage inside the large box with the flap at the back, resting on the base of the box, and the front resting on the bottom of the stage opening. If necessary, trim the back flap so that the stage lies flat.

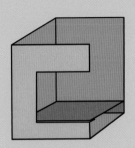

9 Stand the shape on the stage with a gap behind it. Use tape or glue to fix it in place. This creates a back wall with a backstage area behind it.

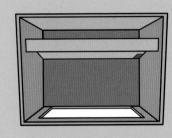

7 Use strong sticky tape or glue (or both) to fix the stage in place. Measure out and cut another piece of cardboard the same width as the stage and about 25 cm tall.

10 Cut six 4-cm-wide strips of cardboard the same height as the back wall. Glue or tape them along the sides of the stage, angled towards the back. These are the wings.

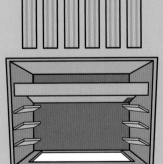

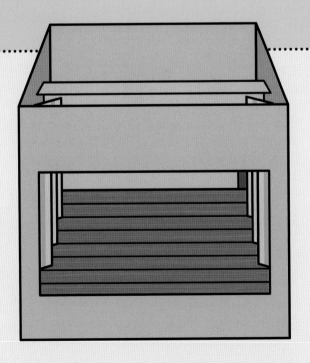

TAKE IT FURTHER ...

If you like, draw lines on the stage to look like floorboards.

THE SWISH OF THE CURTAIN

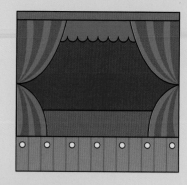

No theatre would be complete without a stage curtain! The curtain opens for the show to begin and closes at the end. Traditionally, theatre curtains are a dramatic deep red, but you can make yours any colour.

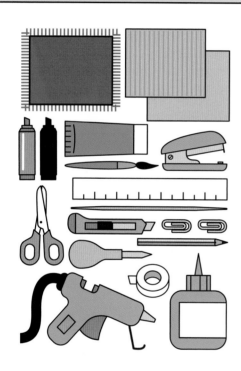

WHAT YOU NEED

- A piece of fabric, the same height as your theatre and about twice as wide
- A stapler
- A skewer or knitting needle as long as the width of your theatre
- A bradawl or thick needle
- Two metal paper clips
- Corrugated or thick card
- Smooth plain card
- Strong scissors or a craft knife
- A pencil and a ruler
- Strong sticky tape
- Strong glue or a glue gun
- Paints and paintbrushes, felt-tip or marker pens (optional)

TIP

Use a light fabric such as thin cotton or linen for the curtains. If you don't want to buy fabric, you could cut up an old unwanted item of clothing, a sheet or tea towel (ask first!).

1 Spread out your fabric and cut it in half. Fold over the bottom and sides of each piece and staple the hem in place.

2 Fold over 2–3 cm along the top of each piece. This fold needs to be larger than the knitting needle or skewer. Staple the fabric down along the edge.

3 Cut four 3-cm-wide and 7-cm-long pieces of thick card. Cut one end of each piece into a curve. Glue the pieces together in pairs.

4 Use a bradawl or thick needle to make a hole through the curved end of each shape. Use strong tape to fix the other ends to each side of the theatre, near the top.

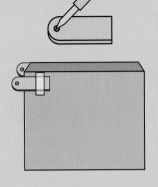

5 Push the knitting needle or skewer through one of the holes, then through the top of both the curtain pieces, then through the other hole. Check the curtains can open and close.

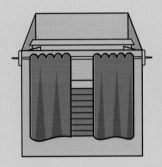

6 Bend the two paper clips into U-shapes. Stick the straight ends into the sides of the stage, between the corrugated card layers. Fix them with glue, to make hooks that hold the curtains open.

7 Cut a large piece of card, slightly longer than the width of the theatre and about 20 cm wide. Fold it into three sections to make a table shape.

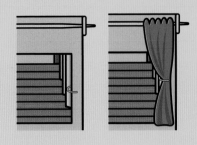

8 Cut two slots in the back fold, so that it can fit onto the sides of theatre and over the curtain. Cut two smaller strips of card and fix them to the ends to make a box shape.

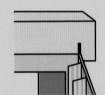

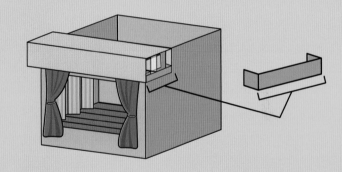

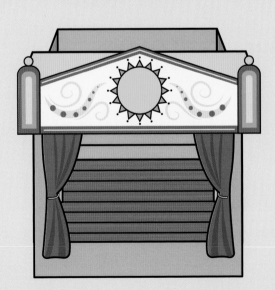

TAKE IT FURTHER ...

You can leave the curtain like this or for a traditional look, cover it with a proscenium arch.

Cut a large arch or triangle shape big enough to cover the front of the box shape. Decorate it with paints or pens, leave to dry. Glue in place.

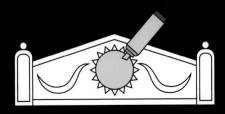

IN THE SPOTLIGHT

Make one, two or more of these moving spotlights
to light up your productions.

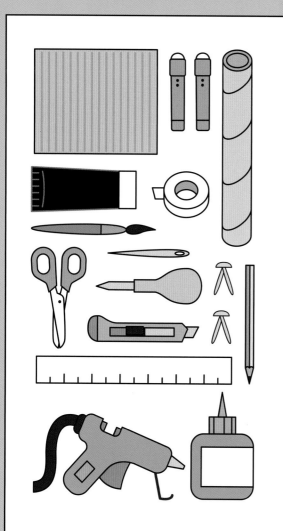

1 Cut two long strips of corrugated card, 2 cm wide. Make them as long as the distance between the front and back of your stage, plus an extra 3 cm.

2 Fold down the extra 3 cm at the end of each strip. Fit the strips along the top sides of your stage, with the flat end resting on the top edge of the back wall and the folded end against the front of the theatre, so that the strips are above the wings.

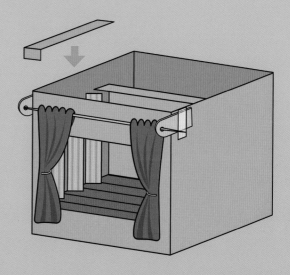

3 If the wings are too tall, trim them down. Glue or tape the strips in place. This space above the wings is the fly loft.

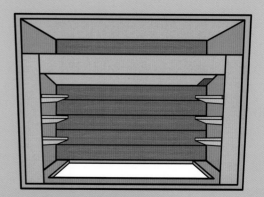

WHAT YOU NEED

- Strong corrugated cardboard
- Two or more small battery-operated torches
- A cardboard tube
- Split pin paper fasteners
- Bradawl or large needle
- Strong scissors or a craft knife
- A pencil and a ruler
- Strong sticky tape
- Strong glue or a glue gun
- Black paint and a paintbrush (optional)

4 Cut a short, thick strip of card to fit across the corner between a side strip and the back wall. Trim the ends at an angle to fit the space. Glue or tape it down.

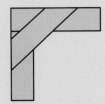

5 Cut another strip of card 2 cm wide and about 10 cm long. Tape one end to the middle of a torch. Wrap the rest tightly around it.

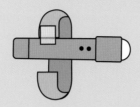

6 Near the end of the strip, make two holes in the card on opposite sides of the torch. Push a split pin through each hole, pointing outwards. Tape down the end of the card strip.

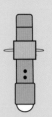

7 Cut a piece of cardboard tube 2 cm long. Cut it in half to make two U-shapes. Glue one inside the other for extra strength. Cut the ends into rounded shapes.

8 Make a hole in the middle of the U-shape and a hole near each end. Push a split pin down through the middle hole. Make a hole in the middle of the corner piece and fix the U-shape to it using the split pin, so that it can turn around.

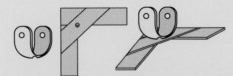

9 Fit the torch into the U-shape and attach the sticking-out split pins to the side holes. It should now be able to point in all directions. If you like, paint the cardboard parts black. Repeat steps 4–9 to add more lights.

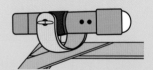

THE SCIENCE BIT!

In the 1800s, theatres lit the stage by heating a chemical called quicklime, making it glow with a light known as 'limelight'. Today, theatre lights are electric, but we still use the term 'in the limelight'!

TAKE IT FURTHER ...

Lights along the front of the stage are called 'footlights'. You could make some with a string of small, battery-powered fairy lights.

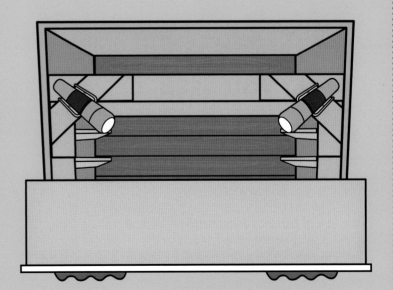

SET DESIGN

Theatre set design brings the stage to life, whether the scene is a desert island, a fairytale palace or a spooky forest at night.

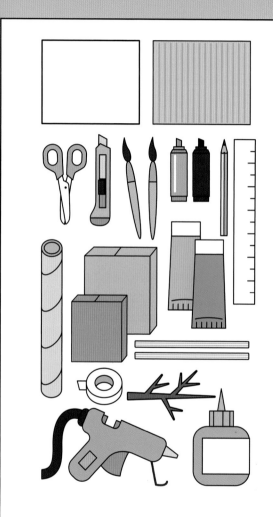

WHAT YOU NEED

- Sheets of smooth, plain white card
- Thicker stiff or corrugated card
- Strong scissors or a craft knife
- A pencil and a ruler
- Strong sticky tape
- Strong glue or a glue gun
- Felt-tip pens or paints and paintbrushes
- Small boxes, tubes, straws (optional)
- Small branching twigs (optional)
- Modelling clay (optional)

1 Cut a slot in the fold at the top of the back wall, so that different set backdrops can be slotted into place. Make the slot about as thick as a pencil and the full length of the back wall, up to the side strips.

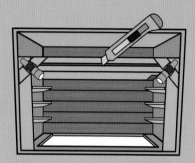

2 Measure the length of the slot, and the height of the back wall. Cut pieces of smooth, white card that are not quite as wide as the slot, but slightly taller than the back wall. These will be your backdrops.

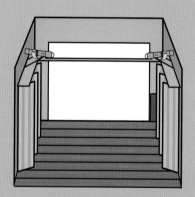

3 Cut several U-shaped tabs from card. Glue one to the top of each backdrop to make a holder. Use pens or paints to create a different scene on the front of each backdrop. Here are some ideas ...

4 Once your backdrops are done (and dry if they are painted!) you can slot them in and out at the back of the stage. You can also line up several backdrops in order, so that you just have to remove the front one to change the scene.

THE SCIENCE BIT!

Although we all know a backdrop isn't real, a good design tricks the eyes of the audience into seeing a 3D scene. To do this, make some objects in the backdrop look further away by making them smaller and fainter.

TAKE IT FURTHER ...

Sets don't have to be realistic – some set designers use abstract shapes and colours to create a particular mood or atmosphere. Try this too!

5 You can also make furniture and other 3D items as part of your theatre sets. Just remember they can't be fixed down, as you have to move them to change scenes. Here are some ideas:

Furniture

Make items like chairs, tables, a sofa or a bookshelf from pieces of cardboard glued together and painted, or using small packaging boxes. Remember to make them the right size for your actors (see page 14)!

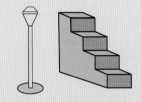

3D scenery

If you have a scene with pillars, railings, lampposts or steps leading offstage, you can add these too. Make them from cardboard, small boxes, tubes or straws. Fix them to a flat base, so they'll stand up by themselves.

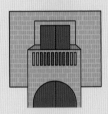

Trees

The easiest way to make trees is to find small, branching twigs. Wash off any mud and let the twigs dry. Fix to a flat base using brown modelling clay. You can also glue on paper leaves.

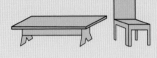

A balcony

For a building with a balcony, draw or paint the building on your backdrop. Then make a balcony using a box, decorated to match the backdrop, and stand it in the right place.

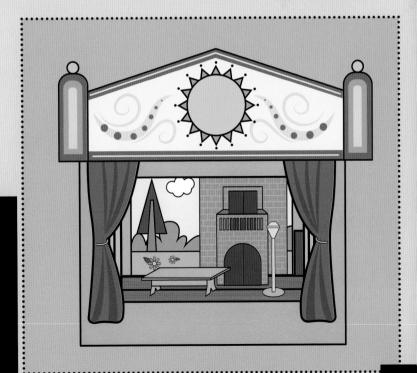

STARS OF THE STAGE

To put on a show you need actors! There are several types of characters you can make for your theatre: paper puppets, toy figures or modelling clay characters. You can combine them too – for example by using toy figures along with a paper puppet dragon or ghost.

For paper puppets:

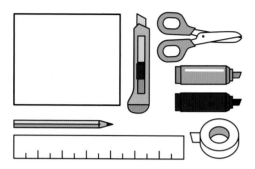

WHAT YOU NEED

- Smooth plain white card
- Strong scissors or a craft knife
- Felt-tip pens
- A pencil and a ruler
- Sticky tape

1 Draw your characters onto card. Colour them in. Make sure they are all to the same scale and fit on the stage. Cut them out, leaving a 2-cm-deep tab at the bottom.

2 cm

2 Cut out strips of card 2 cm wide and as long as the width of your stage. Fold over each character's tab and tape it to the end of a card strip.

For toy figures:

WHAT YOU NEED

- Small plastic or wooden toy figures
- Smooth plain white card
- Strong scissors or a craft knife
- A pencil and a ruler
- Sticky tape or double-sided tape

1 Cut out strips of card 2 cm wide and as long as the width of your stage. Stand a toy figure on the end of each strip and fix down with sticky or double-sided tape.

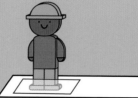

For modelling clay figures:

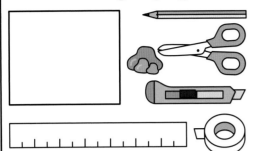

WHAT YOU NEED

- Plasticine or other modelling clay
- Smooth plain white card
- Strong scissors or a craft knife
- A pencil and a ruler
- Sticky tape or double-sided tape

1 Use modelling clay to make your characters. This takes time, but you can make them look exactly how you want to. It also works well for making animals.

2 Cut out strips of card 2 cm wide and as long as the width of your stage. Stand a character on the end of each strip and fix down with sticky or double-sided tape.

To make the characters move:

Cut slots in the sides of your theatre at stage level, big enough for your characters and paper strips to fit through. You can now hold the strips and move the characters around on stage.

TIP

You can also use your characters to make an animation, especially clay figures or toy figures with moving parts. See page 24 to find out how.

TAKE IT FURTHER ...
Add extra detail and special effects with these ideas:

Costumes
It's tricky to make tiny costumes from real fabric, but tissue paper works well. Cut out shapes to make dresses, capes or cloaks. Wrap them around characters and fix with tiny bits of tape.

Props
Small toy or doll's-house items make good props, such as teapots, swords or lamps. Or make them yourself: a cut-up straw for cups or a telescope, a bottle lid for a shield or a cocktail stick for a spear.

Fake blood
To make fake blood, mix a teaspoon of icing sugar, half a teaspoon of water, a pinch of cocoa powder and a few drops of red food colouring. Take care on stage – it's messy!

FLY SYSTEM

If you want your characters to fly like a bird (or even a fly!), you need a fly system. It fits above the stage in the fly loft and controls flying harnesses and ropes.

WHAT YOU NEED

- Two wooden skewers
- A small metal ring, such as a jump ring or split ring from a hobby shop
- A larger metal ring, such as a keyring
- Strong glue or a glue gun
- Strong sticky tape
- Scissors
- Strong thread or thin string
- Invisible thread or fine sewing thread in a dark colour

Jump rings and split rings are used for jewellery making, and are very cheap. But if you can't get one, you can make a small ring by unbending a metal paper clip and winding it around a pen.

Jump Ring   Split Ring   Paper clip Ring

1 Use glue to fix the small ring to the side of one end of a skewer. When it's dry, use strong thread or thin string to tie it on tightly as well, for extra strength.

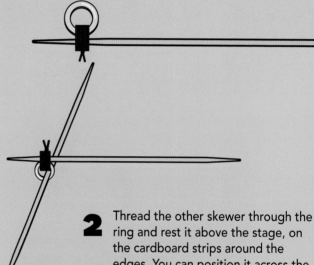

2 Thread the other skewer through the ring and rest it above the stage, on the cardboard strips around the edges. You can position it across the middle or at an angle.

3 Use strong tape to fix the ends of the skewer to the cardboard strips. You should now be able to move the skewer with the ring back and forth along the fixed skewer.

4 Cut a 90-cm-long piece of invisible thread or sewing thread. Thread one end through the small ring and pull it down onto the stage. Tie the other end to the large ring.

5 Tie the loose end of the thread into a loop, so that you can hook it around a character under their arms. (Remove characters from their cardboard strips before making them fly!)

6 Holding the large ring and the loose skewer, you can now make the character fly up and down and move to and fro at the same time.

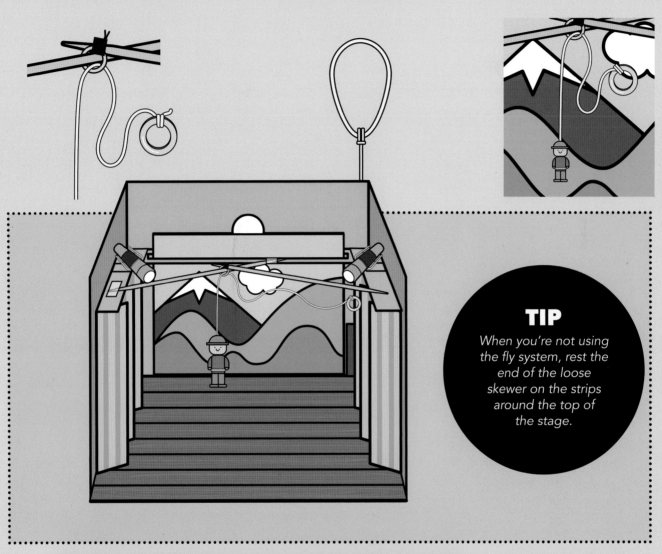

TIP

When you're not using the fly system, rest the end of the loose skewer on the strips around the top of the stage.

TAKE IT FURTHER ...

This is a simple fly system, but you could try making a more complex one. Use wire instead of a skewer to make a curved or bendy flight path, or make two systems so that two characters can fly at the same time. Besides characters you could make other things fly, too. What about a dragon, a rocket or a flying carpet?

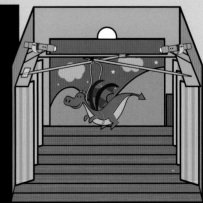

GONE IN A PUFF OF SMOKE!

In movies, it's easy to make characters disappear. But in the theatre, you can only do this with the help of some clever tricks.

WHAT YOU NEED

- A pencil and a ruler
- Scissors and a craft knife
- A bradawl or thick needle
- Strong string
- A thick elastic band
- Strong sticky tape
- Several bendy straws
- Cornflour or cornstarch powder
- A small bowl
- A plastic or rubber squeezy pipette or dropper

You can buy plastic pipettes at a pharmacy, or use the dropper from an old bottle of eye or ear drops. Ask an adult to wash and dry it well first.

1 Cut a wide opening out of the back of your theatre, below the level of the stage. This will let characters exit after falling through the stage.

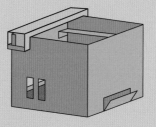

2 Carefully, lie the theatre on its front, and make two cuts into the base, from the edges of the opening, down to the front of the theatre. This flap lets you reach underneath the stage. This is the trap room.

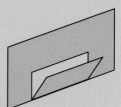

3 Mark a 4-cm square on the stage. Carefully cut along the edge nearest the front of the stage and the two sides.

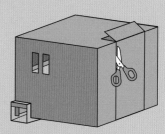

4 Bend the flap downwards to make a trap door. Use the bradawl, skewer or thick needle to make a hole in the flap, not too close to the edge.

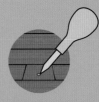

5 Cut a 40-cm piece of string. Tie one end into the hole in the trap door, with the knot underneath. Lead the string under the stage and out of the back of the theatre.

6 Cut the elastic band to make a strip of elastic. Stretch this over the underside of the trap door, near the front. Use strong tape to hold it in place on both sides.

7 Test the trap door by pulling the string. It should open, then close again when you stop pulling. Stand a character on the trap door and test it again, to check they fall through.

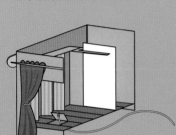

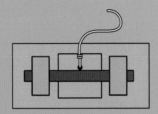

8 Cut a small hole in the stage, about 2 cm in front of the trap door. From below the stage, push the short bendy end of a bendy straw into the slot. Glue or tape it in place, level with the stage. Make sure not to block the hole.

9 Fold the other end of the bendy straw and push it into another straw to fix them together. Seal the join with tape. The straw should stick out of the opening at the back of the theatre.

10 Put some cornstarch powder into a bowl. Use the pipette or dropper to suck some of it up and carefully drop it into the straw in front of the trap door. Do this several times.

11 Now stick the pipette or dropper into the other end of the straw, behind the theatre. Squeeze it hard to make a 'puff' of smoke appear in front of the trapdoor.

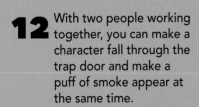

12 With two people working together, you can make a character fall through the trap door and make a puff of smoke appear at the same time.

PEPPER'S GHOST

How can you make a spooky, transparent ghost appear on stage in front of a live audience? In 1862, Henry Dircks and John Henry Pepper developed this amazing trick, which is now called 'Pepper's ghost'.

WHAT YOU NEED

- A ghost character, such as a toy ghost figure or ghost clay model
- Another character to be scared by the ghost
- A small torch, or a theatre spotlight if you've made one
- A piece of clear, stiff acetate, about half the size of your stage

If you don't have a ghost figure, you can make one by covering a toy figure with a piece of tissue paper and drawing on spooky eyes.

You can buy acetate sheets at a hobby store. Or if you have some stiff, clear plastic packaging, you may be able to cut a large enough piece from that.

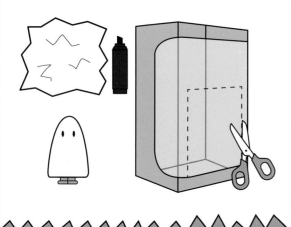

1 Stand your ghost in the wings on one side of the stage, so that you can't see it by looking at the front of the theatre.

2 Fold over about 2 cm at one end of your piece of acetate, so that it can stand up by itself. Stand it on the stage next to the ghost at a 45° angle.

3 Dim the lights in the room you are in and shine a spotlight or torch onto the ghost in the wings. Avoid shining the light through the acetate – shine it from above or from one side.

4 The lit-up ghost will be reflected on to the acetate. Because of the angle, the audience will see the reflection, but they will also see through the acetate, making a transparent ghost.

THE SCIENCE BIT!

The acetate acts like a mirror, but it's also see-through. This means that the audience sees the reflection without seeing the acetate itself. Reflections always hit a mirror and then bounce off it at the same angle. So putting the acetate at a 45° angle makes the ghost's image turn a corner and shine out at the audience.

TIP

Ask someone else to be the audience and look at the stage while you arrange the ghost and acetate. They can tell you when you've positioned everything perfectly and the ghost appears in the right place.

TAKE IT FURTHER ...

For a scary haunting scene, make a spooky haunted house backdrop too. Make the other character or characters on stage look scared or run away!

CINEMA PROJECTOR

Like many real-life theatres, your theatre can also be used as a cinema. All you need is a screen to show movies on, a projector and a smartphone that can play videos.

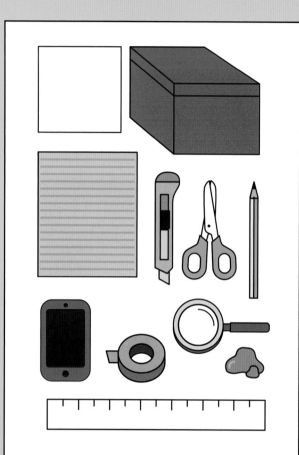

WHAT YOU NEED

- Smooth white card
- A medium-sized rectangular box with a lid, such as a shoebox
- A round magnifying glass, about 6–8 cm across.
- Thick corrugated card
- A pencil and a ruler
- Scissors or craft knife
- Strong opaque (non-see-through) sticky tape, such as duct tape
- Sticky tack or modelling clay
- A smartphone

1 Hold the magnifying glass against one end of the box, with the lens in the middle, and draw around it. Cut out the circle slightly inside the line to make a tight fit.

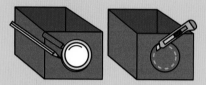

2 Fit the magnifying glass into the hole from the inside of the box, with the handle on the inside. Sticky tape the handle and frame in place, so that any gaps are blocked.

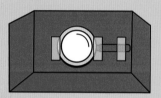

3 Measure and cut out a strip of thick card the same length as the width of the box and 5 cm across. Put it down flat in the box and check it can slide backwards and forwards towards the lens.

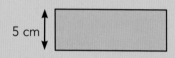

5 cm

4 Measure and cut out another strip of card the same length. Its width should be slightly less than the height of the box. Fix it to the first strip at right angles using tape. This is the stand. Fit the stand into the box and check it can still slide backwards and forwards.

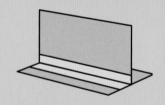

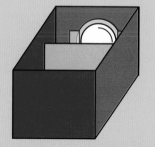

5 Stick two large lumps of sticky tack or modelling clay to the back of your smartphone. Attach it to the stand, on its side, facing the magnifying glass.

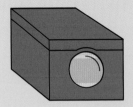

6 Put the lid on the box to make sure it fits. If not, trim off the top of the sticking-up piece of card. If the lid covers part of the magnifying glass, cut that section out of the lid.

7 Set up the phone to play a video or show a still photo. Turn the brightness to maximum and turn off auto-rotate so that when the phone is inside the box, the picture is upside down.

8 Measure the front of your theatre, behind the curtains. Cut a piece of plain white card to fit. Fix it to the front of the theatre with sticky tack or a little tape, to make a screen.

9 Dim the lights or close the curtains in the room. Set up the projector facing the screen, about 1–2 m away. It should be on a flat surface, level with the theatre.

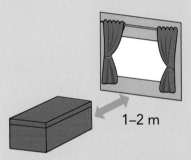

1–2 m

10 Take off the lid and slide the phone backwards and forwards until the picture focuses sharply on the screen. If it doesn't work, try moving the projector nearer or further away too. Once it's working, start the movie.

TAKE IT FURTHER ...

You can also use the projector to create a backdrop, such as waves, projected onto a blank card at the back of the stage.

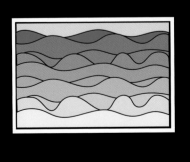

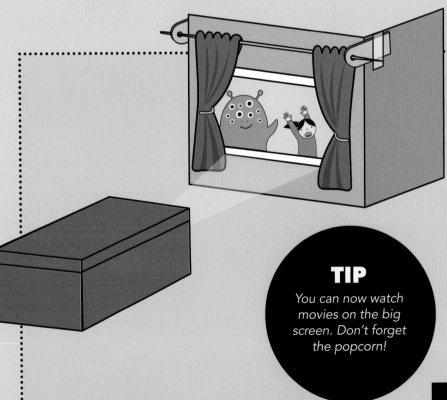

TIP

You can now watch movies on the big screen. Don't forget the popcorn!

23

STOP-MOTION MOVIE

Besides writing plays and performing them in your theatre, you can use it as a setting for a stop-motion animation film, featuring your characters. Or you can make an animation in another setting and show it on your cinema projector.

WHAT YOU NEED

- Characters (toy figures, paper puppets or modelling clay characters)
- A smartphone or tablet
- A stop-motion animation app (see box)
- A tripod or phone stand, or some books and modelling clay
- A pencil and paper
- Theatre with backdrops, props and scenery (optional)

TIP

How does it work? An animation is made up of a series of frames, or shots. In each frame, the characters should change position slightly. When you run the animation, they appear to move.

Animation Apps

With the help of an adult, search for apps that work with your operating system and have good reviews. Some of them are free, while others don't cost much. Here are some suggestions:

For Android:
- Clayframes
- PicPac
- Stop Motion Studio

For Apple:
- iMotion
- I Can Animate
- Stop Motion Studio

1 First write down or sketch what will happen in your movie. Keep it simple at first, as it takes a long time to make a short film. For example, it could be about a dog chasing a cat or someone opening a mystery box to reveal a surprise.

2 Get together all the characters, scenery and anything else that will feature in the story. If you're using modelling clay, make the characters you need.

3 Set up your theatre stage or any other setting such as a flat table. It's best to make your animation indoors in artificial light, as sunlight can change quickly, affecting your scenes.

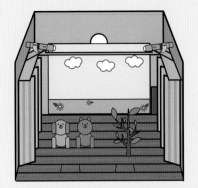

4 Follow the instructions or tutorials to learn how to use your app. Then set up your phone or tablet on the tripod or stand, pointing at the scene where the action will happen.

5 If you don't have a tripod or stand, you can use piles of books and some sticky tack to hold the phone still while you make your animation.

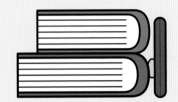

6 Start positioning your characters and taking shots, moving the characters for each new frame. Remember the frames will be speeded up, so only move them a little at a time.

7 Your app will have an 'onion skin', which shows the previous frame faintly, at the same time as the current one. This helps you see how much you are moving the characters.

8 When you've finished, you'll be able to play back the whole animation. Your app should also allow you to add recorded sounds, such as speech, music and sound effects.

THE SCIENCE BIT!

Your animation is made up of a series of still pictures, which don't move. But when we see a sequence of pictures very quickly, in the right order, our brain sees them as movement. This is how all films, cartoons, TV shows and games graphics work.

THEATRE HOUSE

The 'house' is the large theatre building around the stage. It includes the auditorium (where the audience sits), the dressing rooms and the 'front of house' area. This is where you'll find the box office (ticket office) and the bar, where you can buy snacks and drinks.

WHAT YOU NEED

- Large piece of strong corrugated card (this could be from a large cardboard box)
- Lots more strong corrugated card
- Cardboard boxes of various sizes
- Scissors or a craft knife
- Strong glue or a glue gun
- Sticky tape
- Paints and paintbrushes
- Paper clips (optional)
- Foil, stickers, fabric and other decorating materials (optional)

1 Start with a large rectangle of cardboard, at least twice as big as your theatre. Sit your theatre at one end of the rectangle, facing the other end.

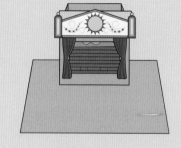

2 Mark diagonal lines leading inwards from the sides of the theatre towards the front end of the cardboard, making a wide funnel shape. Cut out the shape.

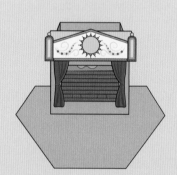

3 Cut two strips of card 12–13 cm wide and the same length of the diagonal lines. Fold over one edge of each strip. Glue these edges under the diagonal sides to make walls.

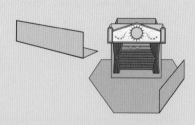

4 Find a medium-sized box that fits next to the theatre at the back. Cut the top off to make low walls. Use pieces of card to divide the space into dressing rooms and a corridor.

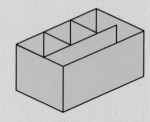

5 Cut a door flap for each dressing room and a stage door at the back end of the corridor. Cut a door through the side of the theatre at stage level, leading into the backstage area.

6 Fold a strip of card in a zig-zag pattern to make steps. Tape it to the wall to link the backstage area to the dressing rooms.

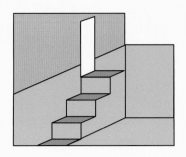

7 Make another set of dressing rooms for the other side of the stage. If you like, make furniture and foil mirrors for the dressing rooms too, with gold star stickers for the doors.

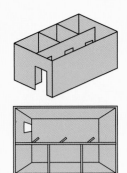

8 Cut 3-cm-wide strips of card. Fold them lengthways to make a row of seats. Sit each row of seats on 2-cm-wide strip of card. If you like, you can also add little armrests made from card or paper clips.

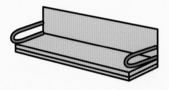

9 Arrange rows of seats in a curved shape around the stage.

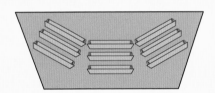

10 Find a larger box that fits on to the narrow end of the funnel shape. Cut doors at the sides to lead into the auditorium and large main doors at the front.

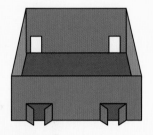

11 Fit a long, narrow box such as a toothpaste box between the two doors with a space behind it, and divide it with a piece of card to make a box office and a bar.

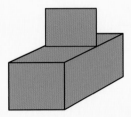

12 Use glue or tape to fix everything in place. Decorate the house with paints or pens. You could also add fabric carpets, a sign above the front doors and even some toilets!

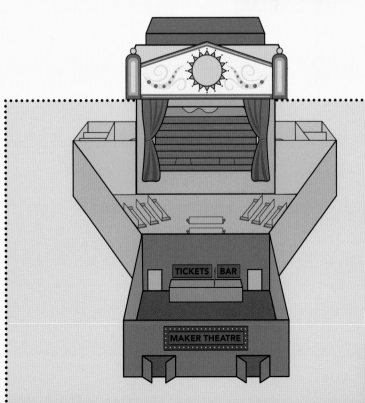

TICKETS BAR

MAKER THEATRE

AND HERE IS YOUR FINISHED THEATRE!

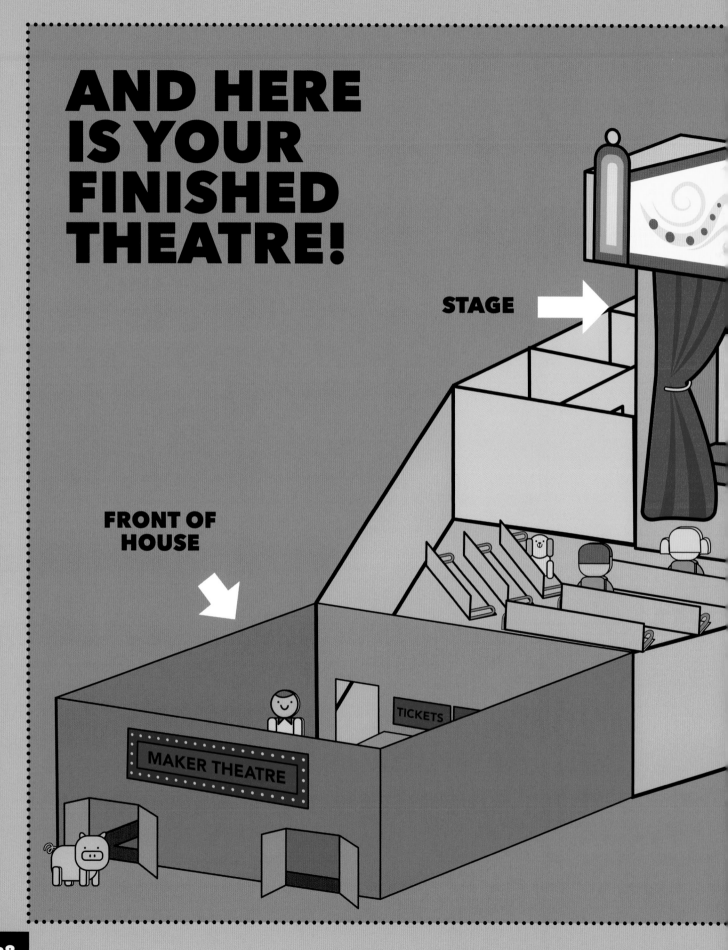

STAGE

FRONT OF HOUSE

MAKER THEATRE

TICKETS

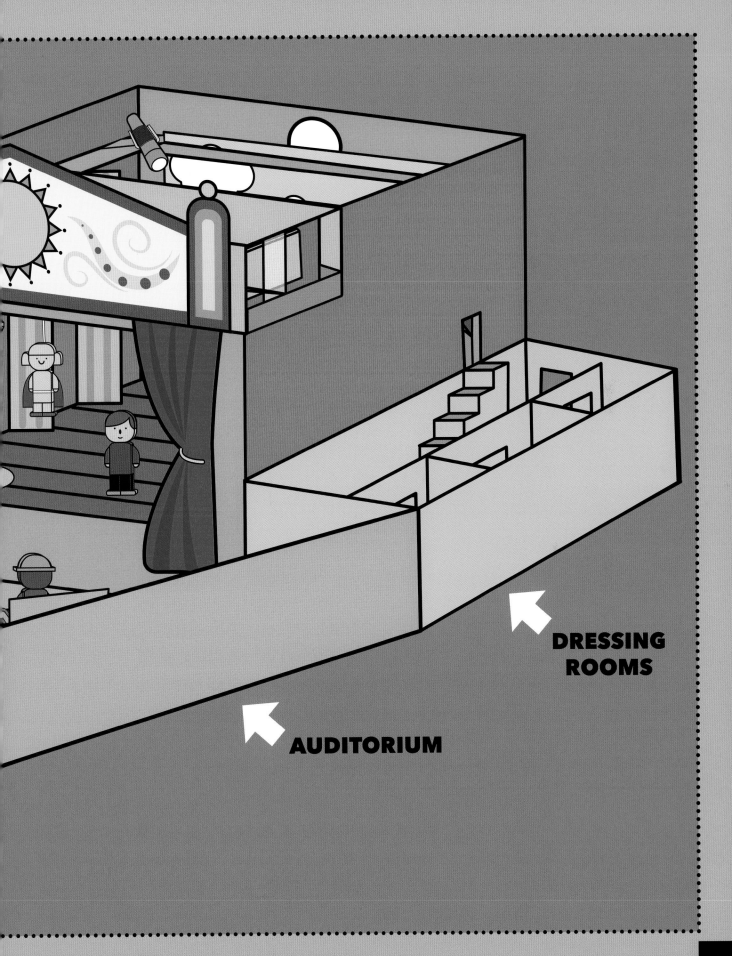

DRESSING ROOMS

AUDITORIUM

GLOSSARY

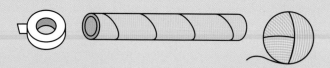

Abstract Made up of shapes, patterns and colours instead of showing real objects.

Acetate Thin, clear, stiff plastic used in packaging, or available at hobby stores.

Auditorium The part of a theatre were the audience sits.

Backdrop A painted scene hung at at the back of a stage.

Backstage. The area behind the stage.

Bradawl A sharp, pointed tool for making neat holes.

Corrugated having parallel rows of folds that look like a series of waves when seen from the edge.

Footlights A row of small lights along the front of the stage.

Fly loft The space above the stage area.

Fly system A system for lifting actors or objects to make them fly around the stage.

Frame One in a series of still images that make up an animation.

Glue gun A gun-shaped electric tool that heats up and applies strong glue.

House The building a theatre is in, or any area apart from the stage, such as the auditorium and box office.

Invisible thread Very thin, fine plastic thread that is hard to see.

Jump ring A small ring made from a piece of curved wire, with unattached ends that can be opened up.

Limelight A type of old-fashioned theatre, light made by heating a chemical called quicklime.

Offstage Out of view of the audience – for example, backstage or in the wings.

Projector A device that projects (or sends out) light to make an image or moving image appear on a screen.

Prop A moveable object used by actors on stage.

Proscenium arch An archway or frame over the front of the stage.

Score To press into card or paper in a line to make it easier to fold.

Set Scenery, backdrops and props used to represent the place and time that the action on stage takes place in.

Split pin A metal fastener, shaped like a pin with two flat spikes that can be opened out to hold the pin in place.

Split ring A small metal ring made of a piece of curved wire that overlaps itself.

Spotlight A theatre light that shines a bright spot of light onto an actor or area of the stage.

Stop-motion animation A way of making animated movies by moving models and objects into different positions, and taking a separate picture for each frame.

Trap room The space under the stage, which can be entered through a trap door in the stage.

Wings Offstage areas at the sides of the stage where actors can wait out of view.

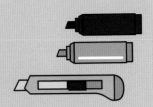

FURTHER INFORMATION

WHERE TO GET MATERIALS

Everyday items
You'll probably have some everyday items and craft materials at home already, such as foil, pens, tissues, string, paper and card, sticky tape, glue and scissors.

Recycling
Old packaging that's going to be thrown away or recycled is a great source of making materials, such as cardboard boxes, yoghurt pots, ice cream tubs, cardboard tubes, magazines, old wrapping paper and newspaper.

Supermarkets
Great for basic items you might not have at home, such as paper cups, cotton wool, a sewing kit, paper straws, wooden skewers and battery-powered fairy lights.

Outdoors
Collect things like leaves, twigs, acorns and seashells for free!

Specialist shops
Hobby and craft shops, sewing shops, art shops, garden centres and DIY stores could be useful for things like a craft knife, a glue gun, acetate, modelling clay, fabric, sand and pebbles. If you don't have the shop you need near you, ask an adult to help you look for online shops, such as Hobbycraft.

Charity shops
It's always a good idea to check charity shops when you can, as they often have all kinds of handy household items and craft materials at very low prices.

BOOKS

All About Theatre by the National Theatre, Walker Books, 2017

Animation Lab for Kids by Laura Bellmont, Quarry Books, 2016

How to Create Animation in 10 Easy Lessons by Will Bishop-Stephens, QED Publishing, 2016

Junk Modelling by Annalees Lim, Wayland, 2016

You Can Work in Theatre by Samantha S. Bell, Raintree, 2019

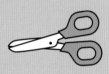

WEBSITES

PBS Design Squad
https://pbskids.org/designsquad/
Lots of brilliant design and build challenges.

DIY
https://diy.org/
An online maker community for kids.

Parents.com Arts & Crafts
https://www.parents.com/fun/arts-crafts/
Maker projects, instructions and videos.

Kiwico DIY page
https://www.kiwico.com/diy/
Fun and easy maker ideas.

INDEX